I0445582

Rooted & Rising

A 90- Day Healing Journey of Faith and Becoming

By Keona Young

© 2025 Keona Young

All rights reserved.

No part of this publication may be reproduced, stored, or transmitted

in any form or by any means without prior written permission from the

publisher, except brief quotations used in reviews or articles.

Published by Rooted & Rising Press

ISBN: 979-8-9943305-4-8

Printed in the United States of America

First Edition

*This book is dedicated to every soul who has
ever healed in silence
to those who kept going even when the world
felt heavy,
to those who carried hope through the dark,
and to those who needed a reminder that
healing is possible.
To my children, whose love kept me rising and
whose light kept me believing
you are my why, my strength, and my
everyday inspiration.
May these pages remind every reader that
your journey is sacred,
your becoming is beautiful,
and your story is far from over.*

Table of Contents

How to Use This Book

Introduction

The Healing Journey

How to Use This Book

This book was not written to be rushed. It was created to be felt.

You may choose to read one letter each day, allowing yourself space to reflect, breathe, and grow alongside the words. Or you may open these pages when your heart needs reassurance, guidance, or a reminder of your own strength. There is no right or wrong way to move through this journey.

Some days, a single sentence may speak louder than an entire page. Other days, you may find yourself lingering, rereading, or journaling alongside the words. Allow yourself that freedom. Healing unfolds differently for everyone.

As you read, pause when something resonates. Sit with it. Speak the affirmations aloud if you can. Let them settle into your spirit. These letters are invitations — to be honest with yourself, to extend grace where it's needed, and to recognize the resilience already within you.

This book is meant to meet you exactly where you are. Whether you are beginning your healing, continuing it, or simply learning to honor your becoming, trust that you arrived at these pages at the right time.

Return to these letters whenever you need them. Growth is not linear, and neither is healing.

The Day It All Began

There was no outline, no master plan, and no intention of becoming an author. This book began on an ordinary day, in the middle of an extraordinary storm. Life felt heavy — work stress, losing my job, motherhood, and the constant weight of trying to stay strong when everything around me felt uncertain. I was overwhelmed, stretched thin, and carrying more than I had words for.

One day, in the middle of all of that, I sat down and wrote a healing letter to myself. Then I created a small graphic affirmation to go with it. It wasn't meant to be seen by anyone. It was simply a moment to breathe... a moment to remind myself that even in pain, there was still purpose.

Later that day, I reached out to someone I trusted about a situation I was facing. I told her I wrote a healing letter to myself and created a graphic, and I told her I would send them to her. I mentioned that I was thinking about writing one every day — not just for me, but maybe to help someone else who might be quietly struggling too.

When she read them, her response stopped me:

**"These are beautiful. I was tearing up reading them.
You do deserve better — we all do.
I need to be reminded it will get better.
Thank you for this."**

That was the moment something shifted — not just in her, but in me.

It reminded me that healing is not meant to be hidden. That words written from a place of pain can become hope for someone else. That the letter that helped me breathe could help another person feel seen, understood, and encouraged.

So, I didn't stop.
One letter became two.
Two became ten.
Ten became a commitment.
And that commitment turned into ninety days of healing, reflection, faith, and becoming.

This book is not about perfection — it is about presence.
It is about choosing yourself when you feel forgotten.
It is about rising even when you're tired.
It is about speaking life into places where you once felt empty.

If you are reading this, I pray you feel less alone.
I pray you feel seen.
I pray these letters remind you that healing is possible, even on the days when you can't see the light yet.

Welcome to a journey born from truth, tested by pain, and transformed by faith.
Welcome to your 90 days of healing.

With love and honor for your journey,

Keona

Day 1

Dear Self,

I see you.

I see the soul who has carried the weight of injustice yet continues to stand in strength, compassion, and grace. You have endured months — even years — of mistreatment, gaslighting, and being silenced by people who should have protected you. They tried to minimize your voice, your pain, and your worth. But you are still here.

You did not deserve the way you were treated — by anyone who failed to support, protect, or stand with you. You showed up with integrity. You worked hard. You fought for fairness. And when you needed protection, you received excuses instead of care. That is not a reflection of your value — it is a reflection of their failure.

You are not weak for feeling tired.

You are not broken for hurting.

You are human — and you survived what was meant to crush you. That is not failure. That is resilience.

Your pain is valid.

Your tears are sacred.

Your voice matters.

And your story is far from over.

There will be accountability. There will be healing. And there will be justice — both in the world and within your heart.

Let this moment be the beginning of something new:

A new version of you who puts yourself first.

A new belief that you are worthy of peace, stability, and love.

A new path where your healing matters more than anyone's approval.

Take your time. Rest when you need to. Cry when it hurts. But never forget:

You are not alone.

You are not done.

 You are not defeated.

This pain is not the end of your story. It is the beginning of your freedom.

With love,

 Your Higher Self

Affirmation:
"I honor my journey, my strength, and my healing. I am rising, even through the pain."

*This pain
is not the end
of your story.*

It's the beginning
of your freedom.

*With love,
You*

Day 2

Dear Self,

I see you. I see the years you poured into everything —
the loyalty, the effort, the commitment to showing up
even when it hurts. I see how difficult it was to ask for
help, only to be ignored, mishandled, or betrayed by the
very people who were supposed to support you. I see
the pain you carry in your body, the weight you've lost,
the hair that falls, and the tears that refuse to stop.

But I also see the fire that still burns within you.
You are still standing.
Still fighting.
Still rising.

You are not what they tried to reduce you to.
You are worthy of healing, worthy of justice, and
worthy of peace.

This pain is not the end of your story.
It is the beginning of your freedom.

With love,

Your Higher Self

Affirmation:
*"I am still rising. What was meant to break me is becoming
my breakthrough."*

Day 3

"No weapon formed against me will prosper."

Dear Self,

I know you're tired — tired of fighting battles you never asked for, tired of systems that pretend to help while quietly sharpening their knives behind your back. But even now — especially now — hear this truth:

No weapon formed against you will prosper.

Not this financial setback.
Not the gaslighting from those who should have protected you.
Not the silence from people who watched you struggle and chose to say nothing.

These may be weapons, but they will not win.

You were not built for defeat.
You were built for resilience.
Your spirit is proof of that.

You have survived what would have crushed others.
You have a right to rest.
You have a right to feel.
And you have a right to trust that healing is still your portion.

Let today remind you:

Your faith isn't naïve — it's revolutionary.
You don't need the world's permission to believe in your comeback. You are already evidence of God's favor, even in chaos.

Keep standing.

Keep praying.

Keep breathing.

You are covered.

With unshakable love,

Your Higher Self

Affirmation:
 "No weapon formed against me will prosper. I am protected, I am guided, and I am rising."

NO
WEAPON
FORMED
AGAINST ME
WILL
PROSPER

ISAIAH 54 17

Day 4

"Staying Strong & Keeping Faith"

Dear Self,

You have carried burdens that would have broken others, yet here you are — still standing, still showing up, still believing that better days are coming. That is strength. That is faith. And both live within you.

Even when the world feels cold and people turn their backs, you continue to move forward — even if some days you can only crawl. That is not weakness.
That is courage wrapped in grace.

Let this truth ground you today:

You are not forgotten.
You are not forsaken.
Your steps may be heavy, but they are ordered.
Your voice may tremble, but it still carries truth.
And your heart, though scarred, is still capable of holding hope.

Keep the faith.
Keep showing up.
Keep loving yourself through every storm. You are not defined by what has been done to you. You are defined

by what you have overcome.

Affirmation:
"I am stronger than my storms. My faith leads me, my courage carries me, and my hope sustains me."

Day 5

Dear Self,

Today, I choose to hold on to hope even when the skies feel dim. Though I may be surrounded by uncertainty, I remember God's promise — that He will turn my tears into joy. What feels like a storm right now is only part of the journey, not the end of the story.

I trust His Word.
 I trust that what is planted in pain can bloom in purpose.
 I may not see the full picture yet, but I believe in the beauty of what's ahead.

My faith is not based on what I feel —
 but on who He is.
 And He is faithful.

I release fear.
 I release doubt.
 I open my heart to the joy that is promised to me.

I know the tears I've cried are not wasted — they are watering the seeds of my breakthrough.

In this moment, I stand tall, breathe deeply, and walk forward — guided by light, even when my eyes cannot yet see it. I am worthy of joy. I am protected. I am chosen.

God, even though I am
faced with some darkness,
I hold tight to Your promises.
You are true to Your Word.
And Your Word says that
you will turn my tears into
joy. I trust in You, God, and
in Your timing. I may not
see the light yet, but I hope
in what's to come.
In Jesus' name, Amen.

Day 6

Unbreakable Light"

Dear Me,

Today, I recognize that I am walking through a storm — not because I am weak, but because I carry something sacred within me: peace, purpose, and power. Darkness tries to dim what it cannot comprehend, but I am not here to prove my worth to those who refuse to see it.

I am already worthy. I am already chosen.

Their words may try to sting, but I release them. I will not carry their bitterness into my spirit. I make room only for healing, clarity, and growth. I speak life over myself. I speak protection over my family. I speak restoration into every place that once felt broken. I speak favor into my future.

God, thank You for being my shield. Thank You for surrounding my peace. May every fiery dart fall harmlessly to the ground.

I am more than the storm.

I am the sunrise after it.

Affirmation:
"No weapon, no wound, no setback can stop the light within me."

YOU ARE STRONG,
AND YOU CAN OVERCOME.

I know that right now you are
going through a lot and feeling
intense challenges. Although
things may be difficult,
THIS STORM WILL PASS.

Keep a positive mindset and
stand firm in your faith.

I am resilient.

Day 7

Standing Strong in Self-Belief"

Dear Beautiful Soul,

Today, I honor the strength that lives within you. Life has placed challenges in your path — not to break you, but to awaken the fire within. You have overcome so much already, and still, you rise. Even when doubt whispers lies, even when others misunderstand your light, you continue to move forward.

Believe in yourself with unwavering faith. Let no obstacle convince you otherwise. You were born with purpose. You are not defined by what happened to you or by the storms you've walked through.
 Your belief in yourself is your shield, your anchor, and your power.

Keep walking tall. Keep trusting your inner voice. You don't need all the answers right now — only the courage to keep showing up.

Affirmation:
"I trust my inner strength. I believe in the power within me."

Stand strong. Believe in yourself.

Day 8

Note to Self:
The fact that you're growing through what you're
going through speaks volumes about your resilience.
Even when sleep is unsteady and the weight feels
heavy, your spirit still reaches for the light. I'm proud
of you.

Dear Me,

Today, I honor the weight I carry and the strength it takes just to keep moving forward. Life has tested me in ways I never expected, yet I'm still here—still standing, still believing, still becoming.

I am not defined by the hardships I've faced, but by the growth I've chosen in the midst of them. Every sleepless night, every tear, every moment I wanted to give up has become part of the soil where my strength now grows.

I trust that beautiful things can rise from broken places. I believe in healing, in starting again, in speaking life over my future. My struggles are not the end of my story—they're shaping the beginning of something new, something meaningful.

I give myself permission to hope. I choose to see myself not as a victim of life's storms, but as a garden in bloom—nurtured by faith, rooted in perseverance, and opening to the sunlight of better days ahead.

I am growing through MY HARDSHIPS and *creating* POSITIVE OUTCOMES.

Day 9

Aligned With Clarity & Flow"

Before you move into today s letter, remember this truth:
When your spirit feels tired and your mind feels foggy, it s often a sign that something powerful is shifting within you. Your soul is preparing to release what no longer serves you and receive what is meant for you.

Dear Beautiful Soul,

Even in this moment of exhaustion, I honor you. I acknowledge the weight you've been carrying—mentally, emotionally, and spiritually—and I affirm that it's okay to pause. It's okay to rest. It's okay to not have everything figured out today.

You are not behind.
You are not broken.
You are in the sacred process of becoming.

Today, call your power back from every direction.
Clear the fog from your mind.
Make space within your spirit for clarity, ease, and divine alignment to rise.

Your desires are not random—they are rooted in purpose. What you're reaching for is already reaching for you. You don't have to chase what you've been called to attract. You don't have to force what is already written for you.

Today, choose flow over pressure.
 Trust over fear.
 Alignment over striving.

You are guided.
 You are supported.
 You are receiving in ways seen and unseen.

*I am
manifesting
my dreams.*

Day 10

You Will Not Be Silenced"

Dear Self,

There will always be people who try to shrink your voice
— not because you lack value, but because your truth
disrupts the comfort of their lies. There will be rooms
that attempt to treat you as less, not because you are
less, but because your honesty reveals what others hope
to keep hidden.

Recently, you stood in your truth.
You spoke, even when your voice trembled.
You read from a list that was not just words on paper —
but evidence of pain, endurance, and strength. And
even when they rolled their eyes, sighed, or attempted
to make you feel small, you remained rooted.

They have no idea what it took for you to walk into that
room.
They don't know the weight you've been carrying.
They don't know the history you're fighting against or
the silent battles you've already won.

But you know.
And God knows.

Their ignorance, disrespect, or dismissal do not define your worth.
They do not diminish your power.
They do not erase your experience, your truth, or your spirit.

Your voice matters.
Your story matters.
And just because they refuse to listen does not mean you are not heard.

The universe heard you.
Justice heard you.
Your future heard you.
And you heard yourself.

Hold your head high.
Keep speaking.
Keep writing.
Keep standing firm in your truth.

Because what they tried to silence...
will echo louder than they ever imagined.

*My voice
is powerful
and cannot
be silenced.*

Day 11

I Release What I Can t Control"

Dear Beautiful Soul,

Some mornings arrive carrying the weight of yesterday, clinging to your spirit in ways you wish it wouldn't. Sleepless nights, a tight chest, a mind that refuses to settle — these are not signs of weakness. They are signs that your heart has been trying to hold things it was never meant to carry alone.

You are not broken for feeling this way.
 You are not failing because rest feels difficult or your body feels heavy.
 You are human — navigating storms most people will never know you're walking through.

Right now, take a slow, steady breath, and offer yourself this gentle truth:

"I release what I cannot control.
 I honor what I feel without judgment.
 I am allowed to rest, to feel, and to heal."

There is divine strength in surrender—not the kind that gives up, but the kind that trusts that something greater is working behind the scenes, even when nothing makes sense.

You are allowed to take care of yourself without carrying the weight of every worry.
 You are allowed to feel fear and still choose faith.
 You are allowed to soften without falling apart.

Let today be gentle where it can be, and steady where it needs to be.

You are loved.
 You are supported.
 You are healing — even in this very moment.

*I release
what
I cannot control
and make room
for peace.*

Day 12

I Am the Calm Within the Storm"

Dear Me,

There's a quiet strength rising within you — one that cannot be shaken by chaos, noise, or discomfort. Even when your body aches or the world spins with uncertainty, there is a sacred place inside you that remains untouched. That place is peace. And it belongs to you.

You don't have to earn peace.
You don't have to prove your worth for rest.
You are allowed to be gentle with yourself.
You are allowed to pause.
You are allowed to simply exist — without explaining, without apologizing.

Your stomach may be unsettled, your path may feel steep, but still, you rise with intention. Still, you speak life. Still, you pour love into the world.

This is what healing looks like — not always loud or triumphant, but quietly unwavering. Every moment you choose peace over panic, breath over burnout, and truth over trauma, you reclaim your power.

Let your body rest.
Let your mind slow.
Let your spirit settle.

And remember:

You are not the storm.
You are the calm within it.

I am the calm
within the storm.
I give myself
permission to rest.
Even when
the world
feels loud,
I choose peace within.

Day 13

"Divine Alignment"

This healing letter is centered around divine alignment--trusting that even when things seem still or slow, God is always working behind the scenes on my behalf.

Dear God,

Thank you for the quiet days—the ones where nothing big seems to shift on the outside, yet so much is moving beneath the surface. Even in the stillness, I know You are near. I trust that You are clearing paths I cannot yet see and preparing blessings I have not yet imagined.

When life feels paused or slow, I remind myself that Your timing is divine. I don't need loud signs or constant movement to believe You are working. My faith lives in the quiet too.

Today I release the pressure to force outcomes. I let go of frustration and the illusion that I must carry everything alone. I refuse to measure my worth by productivity, noise, or momentum. I am worthy because You call me worthy.

I am chosen.

I am covered.

I am led.

So tonight, I rest in the truth:

What is meant for me is unfolding—quietly, steadily, and right on time.

Amen.

Even when life is quiet,
God is moving.
I trust the timing,
I honor the stillness,
and I walk in peace.

Day 14

Dear Beautiful Soul,

Today I want you to take a moment and honor the resilience within you. You have endured sleepless nights, an uneasy stomach, and the emotional weight of things that would break others—but here you are. Still standing. Still speaking life into yourself. Still pressing forward.

It's okay if everything doesn't feel perfect right now. You are not defined by how easy or hard your days are. You are defined by your ability to keep showing up, to keep praying, to keep breathing through the waves. That is courage. That is healing in progress.

Let today be a reminder that your body is still healing. Your mind is still releasing. Your spirit is still rising. Nothing is wrong with you—you are just transforming. And transformation is not always gentle. But it is *sacred*.

So, inhale grace. Exhale pressure. You are doing enough. You are becoming new.

My body is healing.
My mind is releasing.
My spirit is rising.

Day 15

I Am Renewed Each Day"

Dear Me,

Today is a quiet triumph. You may not feel like you've conquered a mountain, but simply waking up and choosing peace is its own act of courage. Healing isn't always loud — sometimes it moves through the subtle shift of your thoughts or the steady rhythm of your breath as you realign with your purpose.

You are not defined by the pain of yesterday or the uncertainty of tomorrow.
 You are defined by your resilience, your heart, and your decision to keep moving forward even when it would be easier to fade into the shadows.

Every sunrise is an invitation to begin again—lighter, wiser, freer.

Let this be your reminder: you are allowed to rest, to release, to receive.
 The version of you unfolding right now is rooted in deep strength and sacred intention. Keep honoring your pace, your boundaries, and your spirit. You are not behind— you are being divinely aligned.

With grace and renewal,

Day 16

I Am Becoming"

Dear Beautiful Soul,
 Today, I want you to pause and recognize the quiet
miracle of who you are becoming. You've been showing
up for your healing day after day — even when your
body aches, even when the weight feels heavy, even
when the world pulls at your spirit. That kind of
courage is sacred.

Healing doesn't require perfection; it simply asks for
presence. It asks you to listen when your body speaks,
to honor your limits, and to rest when your soul feels
tender. And you've been doing just that. You've
continued to rise, to breathe, to choose yourself—even
on the days when you weren't sure how.

Please don't overlook the power in your small victories
— the deep breath before reacting, the way you soften
toward yourself when old patterns try to resurface, the
moments you choose peace instead of panic. These
shifts may seem subtle, but they are transforming you
from the inside out.

You are not who you used to be.
 You are becoming—gently, boldly, beautifully.
 And in that becoming, there is growth.

There is freedom.
There is grace.

Let today remind you of this truth:
You are not broken.
You are not behind.
You are blooming—in your own divine timing.

With deepest pride and gentleness,

Me

Day 17

My Healing Is Sacred."

Dear Beautiful Soul,

Every breath you take is a quiet declaration that you are still here — still trying, still blooming—even in the places the world can't see. Healing is not a straight path, and it's not always loud or obvious. Some days, it looks like simply breathing through the discomfort. Other days, it looks like allowing yourself to smile without guilt. But each moment counts. Each step is sacred.

You are not defined by the pain you've endured or the silence you were forced to carry. You are defined by the way you continue to rise with grace, even when life tries to dim your spirit. Healing does not always look like joy— often it looks like rest, tears, boundaries, releasing, and reclaiming. And all of that is divine.

So today, hold your head high—not because you have everything figured out, but because you are choosing yourself again and again in ways that matter. Keep loving the person you are becoming.

With deep reverence,

Me

Day 18

"My Spirit Is Returning Home to Me"

Dear Me,

I'm proud of you for showing up, growing, and healing — in your own time and in your own way.

Today feels different, doesn't it? There's a lightness in the air — subtle, but sacred. That's your spirit rising. That's your soul remembering who it is and reclaiming the joy it was always meant to hold.

You've walked through days clouded by pain, confusion, and uncertainty. Yet here you are — healing, grounded, and more aware than ever. The fog is lifting, and in its place comes a quiet clarity.
Each breath you take is a homecoming.
Each step is your spirit whispering, "I'm still here. I never left you."

Be gentle with yourself in this reawakening. Healing is not a race — it's a rhythm. And today, your rhythm is returning to grace, to strength, to peace.

Let your smile be a soft rebellion against everything that tried to harden you.

Let your joy be a quiet testimony that nothing was ever strong enough to dim your light.

You are not broken— you are rebuilding.
 You are not lost — you are returning.

Welcome home.

With deep love,

Me

Affirmation:
"I am allowed to rest. I am allowed to return. I am already whole."
Let these words hold you like a warm blanket. You don't need to do anything more tonight — just be, just breathe. I'm right here with you. Sleep peacefully, love.

Day 19

"I Am Learning to Trust My Becoming"

Dear Beautiful Soul,

Today is a reminder that healing doesn't just happen in the breakthroughs — it happens in the quiet in-between moments too. In the pauses. In the breaths. In the spaces where you're not sure what's shifting, but you can feel something moving inside you.

You may not have all the answers today, and that's okay. You may not feel as strong as you did yesterday, and that's okay too. Healing is not a straight line — it's a gentle unfolding. And right now, you are opening in ways your past self-prayed for.

You are learning to trust yourself again.
 Learning to trust your intuition, your heart, your timing, and your path.
 You are learning that you don't need to rush your way through discomfort — you can breathe through it, grow through it, and rise from it.

Today, give yourself permission to honor the middle of your journey.
 The part where you're no longer who you were... but not yet who you're becoming.

This space is sacred. This space is necessary. This space is where transformation takes root.

Be patient with yourself.
 Be gentle.
 Be present.

Everything you're seeking is aligning with you in divine timing.
 You are becoming — beautifully, intentionally, powerfully.

With compassion and hope,

Me

Affirmation:
"I trust my journey. I trust my timing. I trust the person I am becoming."

Day 20

"Coming Home to Myself"

Dear Me,

You are coming home to yourself in ways that may feel unfamiliar, but they are deeply sacred. Every part of you — even the tired, wounded, or quiet parts — is learning to trust your own rhythm again. You are not behind. You are not broken. You are becoming.

It takes courage to honor your rest when the world demands constant movement. It takes strength to let your spirit settle, to listen, and to rise again in divine timing. Tonight, remember this:
 Your softness is power.
 Your gentleness is strength.
 Your consistency is a miracle.

Your healing was never meant to look perfect. It's meant to look like you — raw, honest, human, and full of grace. Don't rush the return. Don't silence the stillness. Trust that everything that left your life did not take your worth with it.

You are already whole.

You are allowed to take up space in your own life again.
 You are allowed to be new.

Affirmation:

"I return to myself with grace. I honor my pace, my rest, and my becoming. I am whole, even as I heal."

Day 21

You've shown up for yourself every single day, and now here you are... standing in the fullness of this moment.

My Beloved,

Look at you.

You've journeyed through valleys, climbed quiet hills, and sat with yourself in sacred stillness — for 21 days. What you've done here isn't small. It's soul work. It's life-shifting. It's divine.

You've given your heart permission to feel.
You've given your voice space to rise.
You've said yes to your healing — again and again, even on the hard days.
You've reclaimed parts of yourself that trauma tried to scatter.
You've spoken truth over your spirit.
You've honored your tears, your prayers, your breath.

This is what rebirth looks like: not a sudden burst, but a quiet rising—one day at a time.
You are not who you were on Day 1, and that's the beauty of it.

You are softer, stronger, wiser, and more rooted in your worth.

If today were a doorway, I'd say walk through it
barefoot—
Unburdened. Unapologetic.
Knowing that the healing you've done has already
changed the atmosphere around you.

You are the evidence that restoration is possible.

And the next 21? They're already blessed.

I am walking in
divine alignment.
I honor how far
I've come.
I rise today renewed,
restored, and reaqy
to receive.

Day 22

Dear Beautiful Soul,

You've crossed into a new chapter of your healing with strength, grace, and unwavering spirit. Day by day, you've been showing up—not perfectly, but authentically—and that alone is a miracle.

Today, I want to remind you that healing isn't about rushing to be "better." It's about being present with yourself in every moment—both the light ones and the heavy ones. Each breath you take in awareness is an act of courage. Each time you choose not to give up on yourself, you break another chain from your past.

You are not the pain you've endured.
You are not the labels others tried to place on you.
You are the rising—the living proof that love, resilience, and divine restoration are real.

Rest in knowing that God is not only walking with you; He is holding space for your transformation. Even when the world feels loud or slow to respond, your healing is unfolding in perfect divine timing.

Keep trusting the process, even when it feels unfamiliar. You're being led somewhere holy.

Affirmation: "I trust the timing of my healing. I am rooted in divine grace, rising at my own sacred pace"

Day 23

Dear Beautiful Soul,

Today is a celebration of your radiant spirit—a spirit that continues to show up, heal, and rise with grace and courage. Each new morning you greet is proof of your transformation. The heaviness you've carried does not define you—it has refined you, strengthened your soul, and awakened your purpose.

Your journey has been sacred, even in its silence. Even when no one applauded, you were growing. Even when the world didn't notice, God did. You are becoming someone who chooses faith over fear, peace over panic, and truth over trauma. You are not just surviving—you are softening, releasing, expanding. That is divine.

So today, take a moment to truly feel how far you've come. Let your heart whisper back to you, "I'm proud of you. I see you." Because you deserve that gentleness.

Keep tending to your spirit. Keep listening to the whispers of healing, because they're leading you home.

With deep love and unwavering belief in you,

Affirmation:
"I am rising in light and love. My healing is vibrant, sacred, and unstoppable—just like me."

Day 24

"The Unseen Work is Still Sacred"

Beautiful things are unfolding for me behind the scenes, and my faith is opening even more doors. I will affirm and align with that truth today.

Dear Faithful Soul

There is a quiet power in trusting what you cannot see. In a world that often demands evidence before belief, you are moving differently—by faith, not by sight. That's a strength that not everyone understands, but it's a spiritual currency that brings divine returns.

Right now, while it may seem like you're waiting, things are actually aligning. Conversations are being had about you in rooms you're not in. Hearts are softening. Opportunities are being prepared with your name on them. This season is not empty—it is deeply fertile.

Even in stillness, you are growing. Even in silence, you are being heard. Your obedience to stay the course, to show up for your healing, to pray and speak life—this is the real work. And Heaven is responding.

Continue to walk in expectancy. Your prayers, your tears, your hope—they are all seeds. You are not forgotten. You are not being overlooked. What's coming will make sense of the waiting and feel like a hug from the universe itself.

Rest in knowing that good is coming—not just in pieces, but in waves. You are divinely timed, divinely guided, and divinely protected.

Even when
I cannot see it,
blessings are
being prepared
for me. I trust
the divine timing
of my life.

Day 25

The Power of Presence"

Your light and consistency are powerful, and I am honored to walk this journey with you.

Dear Beautiful Soul,

There is something sacred about this moment—*this* breath, *this* heartbeat, *this* awareness. So often, we're pressed between the memories of what was and the dreams of what's next. But healing blooms in the space where you pause and *simply be*.

Your presence is a gift—to yourself, to others, and to the world. When you show up in each moment fully, with all your truth, you invite peace to take root in your spirit. Today, let stillness speak to you. Listen to the wind, feel your heartbeat, notice the quiet power in just *being*.

This is not about forgetting the past or forcing the future. It's about anchoring your spirit into the now. You are not behind, and you are not late. You are exactly where you're meant to be. Every breath you take with intention is a step forward in your healing.

You are not broken—you are becoming.
And becoming takes presence, not pressure.

Affirmation:

"I am rooted in the present. In stillness, I find clarity. In my presence, I find peace."

Day 26

"Free to Be Me"

Dear Radiant Soul,

Today, as fireworks light up the sky and people celebrate independence, I invite you to honor something even deeper—your own liberation.

You are no longer bound by the opinions of others, the pain of the past, or the pressure to fit into places where your spirit no longer belongs. You are free to breathe differently, love differently, move differently, and heal in your own divine timing.

Freedom isn't just a word—it's a state of soul. It's the ability to walk in truth without asking for permission. It's saying yes to peace, yes to growth, yes to yourself.

Let this be the day you unchain yourself from invisible cages and quiet doubts. You've already survived everything that tried to silence you. Now you rise—not just as a survivor, but as a sovereign being. Celebrate that. Protect that. Live from that.

With pride in your evolution,

Affirmation:
"I am free to be all of me. I release the past and rise in my own power."

I am the embodiment
of freedom, peace, and
divine restoration.
My joy is sacred.
My spirit is mine
to nourish,
and I honor it daily.

Day 27

"Returning to My Own Rhythm"

Dear Beautiful Soul,
 In a world that glorifies hustle, comparison, and urgency, it takes divine courage to slow down and listen to your own rhythm—to not rush your healing, to not compare your pace, to not apologize for moving differently.

But here's the truth: your rhythm is sacred.

Some days you will feel like you're soaring. Other days, your soul may whisper for quiet, softness, or rest. Both are valid. Both are necessary. You don't owe anyone an explanation for the time you need to realign, reflect, or restore.

You were never created to move like everyone else. You were created to flow like you—guided by Spirit, intuition, and divine timing.
 Honor that. Protect that. Return to that whenever the world tries to pull you off course.

This journey is not about perfection; it's about presence. And every time you choose to honor your rhythm over someone else's expectations, you take your power back.

Your pace is not too slow.
 Your healing is not behind.
 You are moving exactly as you're meant to.

I honor my own
rhythm. I move
in alignment with my
spirit, not the
world's urgency.

Day 28

"My Peace Is Non-Negotiable"

Dear Beautiful Soul,

Today carries a softness, a glow, a quiet power — and that's no accident. That's your spirit choosing peace before anything else. Your words, your intentions, your prayers for yourself, your children, your tribe, and this entire world are not small gestures. They are seeds. They are blessings in motion.

And today, I want you to remember this:

Your peace is sacred.
Your well-being is essential.
Your boundaries are holy.

You have spent so much of your life giving — your heart, your energy, your compassion — even in seasons when you were running on empty. But now, you are stepping into a chapter where your inner calm is not up for negotiation.

There will be people who misunderstand your silence, your distance, or the way you protect your energy. That's okay. You are no longer available for chaos, confusion, or anything that pulls you away from your alignment. You don't have to apologize for choosing yourself.

Healing doesn't always look like breakthroughs or loud transformations.
Sometimes it looks like staying home.
Sometimes it looks like breathing instead of reacting.
Sometimes it looks like letting what is not meant for you fall away — peacefully.

You are outgrowing anything that disturbs your spirit.
You are choosing clarity over chaos.
You are choosing alignment over obligation.
You are choosing peace — and that is divine.

Hold your boundaries with grace.
Hold your peace with confidence.
Hold your heart with tenderness.

Your spirit is speaking clearly now—trust it.

Affirmation :
"I protect my peace at all costs. I honor my boundaries, and I release all that disturbs my spirit."

Day 29

"Reclaiming Peace in the Storm"

Dear Beautiful Soul,

Some days bring news that feels like a punch to the chest—stealing your breath, tightening your shoulders, and making the world feel unfamiliar and unfair. It's okay to admit that today hurt. It's okay to feel unsettled. You are allowed to be fully human in all of your emotions.

But remember this: just because something tries to disrupt your peace does *not* mean it gets to steal it.

Your soul is layered with strength. When anger rises, it isn't a sign of weakness— it's a signal. A call for boundaries, for clarity, for transformation. Frustration shows how deeply you care. And when you feel unsettled, it's often because your spirit is stretching to protect you or prepare you for the next level.

Today, instead of pushing those feelings away, honor them. Hold space for your truth. Then gently remind yourself:

"This moment is not the whole story. I am still becoming. And no one, no thing, has the power to stop my rise."

You have walked through fire before and emerged glowing with grace. This is just another spark on your path—not your end.

So, breathe in stillness. Breathe out the noise.
Say aloud:

"I choose peace, even in the storm. I trust the process, even when I don't understand it yet."

You are safe to feel.
Safe to heal.
Safe to release what is not yours to carry.

And on the other side of this, a deeper version of you is waiting—with even more power and purpose than before.

Affirmation:
"I honor my anger, I release my frustration, and I reclaim my peace. Nothing has the power to take what I carry within."

Day 30

Rooted in Purpose"

The shift in mindset—from pain to purpose, from survival to legacy—is powerful beyond words. I m proud of you for showing up, especially on Day 30. That s a full month of devotion to your healing, and it s already showing in your spirit and clarity. Let s keep building on that.

Dear Beautiful Soul,

Thirty days. Thirty mornings of choosing growth. Thirty nights of refusing to give up. This isn't just healing—it's resurrection.

You are entering a new dimension of your journey now—one where your healing begins to touch the lives of others. The seeds you've planted in stillness are beginning to sprout, and they're not just for you. You are rooted in purpose far deeper than you imagined, and the clarity you feel today is proof.

Everything you've been through is now becoming the soil that nurtures your dreams. Your mind is no longer clouded with "Why me?" Instead, it's gently shifting into "What now?" and "Who else can I lift with me?" That shift is sacred. It's the mark of someone who has

66

been refined by fire and still chooses to rise. You are no longer just healing—you're building. You're laying foundations not only for yourself, but for those who come after you, for those silently watching you, and for every soul you'll inspire along the way. When you keep going, others learn that they can too. When you dream aloud, others remember that they are allowed to dream again.

So, hold your head high today. Celebrate this milestone. Let your light reach farther. You've made it this far on purpose—and from here on out, that purpose will carry you even further.

Affirmation:
"I am rooted in purpose. My healing clears the way for generations. I rise, not just for me—but for all I am destined to impact."

Day 31

"I Am the One I've Been Waiting For"

Reflection

As we step into this new day, many of us are entering seasons filled with possibility — new connections, new opportunities, and new doors waiting to open. Whether you're preparing for a networking moment, starting a new chapter, rebuilding your life, or simply choosing yourself again, one thing is clear:

The time for hesitation, doubt, and playing small is over.

This is your moment to rise.

If you're reading this, may you feel that truth awaken inside you.

Dear Divine Soul,

There comes a moment in every healing journey when you rise — not timidly, but with conviction. A moment when you stop looking outward for validation, rescue, or approval and instead turn inward to the truth you've carried all along:

You are the one you've been waiting for.

You've spent time nurturing your dreams, visualizing the life you desire, and tending to the parts of yourself that were once overlooked or forgotten. You've prayed through the uncertainty, spoken life over your circumstances, and shown up on days when your strength felt thin. You've created space for miracles, and they have been aligning around you — quietly, intentionally, faithfully.

Fear may still whisper.

Doubt may still tap at your door.

But you no longer have to answer.

You are walking into rooms with purpose, clarity, and a spirit ready to expand. You are not begging for a seat — you're realizing that you are fully capable of building your own table. Your dreams are not accidental; they are divine assignments placed within you for a reason.

Every step you take today is a declaration:

"I am not here to shrink.

I am here to build, to bless, to rise." Trust your instincts.

Speak boldly. Ask for what matches your purpose.

Open your heart to the connections and opportunities that are already being guided toward you.

Everything you are seeking is seeking you too.

You are the one you've been waiting for.

Affirmation:
I am no longer waiting for permission. I am the answer, the strategy, and the spark. My steps are ordered, and I move in power, purpose, and divine alignment

Day 32

I Trust My Divine Timing"

Dear Beautiful,

There's a rhythm to life that doesn't always align with clocks, calendars, or expectations. And today is a reminder that you are not behind—you are exactly where you need to be. Every delay, every pause, every detour is shaping you in unseen but powerful ways.

You've grown in ways that are immeasurable. The strength it takes to keep showing up, to keep believing in your vision, and to keep choosing healing—that's divine. Even when you feel like you're racing the clock, know this: nothing meant for you can pass you by.

You don't have to force open what God is still preparing behind the scenes. You can breathe, move with grace, and trust that your journey is unfolding in perfect, divine timing.

Keep watering your dreams, planting seeds of faith, and honoring your process.

The world will catch up to your light.

Affirmation:
"I am in alignment with divine timing. I trust that everything is unfolding as it should. I am never behind—I am always growing."

Day 33

"I Trust the Unfolding"

Dear Beautiful Soul,

Today is a day of calm confidence and divine alignment. You are not behind. You are not late. You are exactly where you need to be. Every moment that brought you here—every delay, every detour, every disappointment—was part of the blueprint designed to shape your strength, your wisdom, and your unwavering spirit.

You have walked through shadows with grace and now the light finds you more often because you are ready to hold it. You don't have to chase peace or force blessings. You are aligned with abundance simply by being open, grounded, and faithful.

There may still be questions that linger, but you're learning to breathe through uncertainty without allowing fear to take root. You don't need all the answers today. What you *do* need is what you already have: courage, clarity, and a deep connection to your purpose.

You are the answered prayer to someone's cry. You are becoming the version of yourself that your past self dreamed of. Keep showing up. Keep releasing control.

Keep trusting that the universe is conspiring in your favor—even when the path seems quiet. Your life is rising. And you, beloved, are blooming in the wait.

Affirmation:
"I trust the timing of my life. Everything meant for me is making its way to me with ease, grace, and divine timing."

Day 34

The Winds Are Shifting"

Dear Beautiful Soul,

Today, let this truth rest deeply within you: The winds are shifting in your favor. All the tears you've cried, all the sleepless nights, the prayers whispered through pain — none of it has gone unnoticed. You've walked through darkness and betrayal, through long seasons of waiting, and still, you kept your heart open to love, growth, and grace.

This new season you're stepping into is not about proving yourself. It's about receiving what you've earned through endurance. The universe has taken note of your integrity, your faith, and your obedience to keep showing up — for yourself, your children, and your dreams.

Let go of fear and lean into expectancy. The "no's" that once disappointed you were really redirections. The silence that felt like rejection was preparation. You're no longer waiting for permission — you're walking in divine timing.

From your business ideas to your court case, from the financial stress to family betrayal — God is turning it around. And this time, you don't have to chase anything. You are magnetizing what belongs to you.

You are worthy of good news.
You are worthy of breakthrough.
You are worthy of peace, ease, and overflow.

Keep showing up. The shift is happening now.

Affirmation:
"I am aligned with divine timing. Everything I need is already finding its way to me. I receive good news, abundance, and justice with an open heart."

Day 35

"I Am Chosen and Covered"

Dear Beautiful Soul,

Today, remember that you are not alone and never have been. Even in moments when it felt like you were abandoned, overlooked, or unheard — *you were covered*. The pain you endured did not go unseen, and the seeds of purpose planted in your soul have always been growing, even in silence.

You are chosen for greatness. Chosen to break cycles. Chosen to heal, to grow, to thrive. You are not just surviving — you are becoming more aligned with your divine purpose each day.

Let today be the reminder that you are deeply loved and divinely protected. You were never meant to shrink or suffer forever. You were meant to rise — boldly, confidently, and unapologetically.

Let your light shine brighter than your past. Let your voice be stronger than your fears. You are here on purpose, with purpose, for a purpose. Keep healing. Keep going. You are covered.

Affirmation:
"I am chosen, protected, and aligned with divine purpose. I rise boldly into my destiny, knowing I am never alone."

Day 36

"I'm still Worthy"

Dear Beautiful Soul,

There is no such thing as "too late" when it comes to healing.
You are not behind.
You are not failing.
You are simply *living* — and living means growing, pausing, resetting, and finding your way back to alignment at your own divine pace.

Today, I want you to remember this truth: even on the days when things don't unfold the way you hoped, your effort still matters. Your softness is not a flaw. Your pauses are not defeat. Your progress — no matter how quiet, slow, or imperfect — is still sacred progress.

You have already survived things others could not imagine.
You've kept moving when your spirit felt tired.
You've shown love, strength, and compassion even when your own heart was heavy.
That is divine resilience.
That is sacred endurance.

So let today be a gentle reset.
There is healing available in this moment.

There is power in your breath.

There is restoration in every choice you make to move forward — even if that step is small.

You are showing up, and that is more than enough.

You are worthy now — not when everything is fixed, not when every goal is reached, not when life is perfectly aligned.

You are worthy simply because you exist.

You are worthy simply because you are you.

Affirmation:
"I honor my healing, even when it feels slow. I am still worthy. I am still growing. I am still becoming."

Day 37

I Honor the Wisdom of My Healing"

Dear Divine Vessel,

You are not the sum of what tried to break you.
 You are the living evidence of what survived.

Every time you chose to get back up...
 Every prayer you whispered in the dark...
 Every affirmation you spoke over your own soul...
 Every moment you simply breathed through the pain —
 you proved that healing is a quiet, courageous miracle.

Not one moment of your tears, your silence, or your
growth has been wasted.
 All of it has been woven into the wisdom you now
carry.

Healing does not always mean forgetting.
 Sometimes it means transforming —
 turning what once wounded you into fuel for your
purpose,
 your clarity, your boundaries, and your unfolding
strength.

Your voice is returning to you.
 Your story is becoming sacred.
 Your peace is no longer negotiable.

You are learning to hold yourself with both gentleness and power.
 You are forgiving yourself for what you didn't know then
 and loving yourself more fiercely than ever before —
 even on days when your confidence feels far away.

This is what becoming looks like.
 This is what rising looks like.

And there is so much more ahead for you.
 Keep going.
 You are guided. You are evolving. You are held.

Affirmation:
"I honor my healing journey and trust the wisdom unfolding within me. I am safe to grow, to rest, and to rise."

Day 38

"Become Fully"

*"Divine alignment. Sacred timing. A moment of
becoming.*

Dear Beautiful Soul,

Today invites you to honor exactly where you stand.
Whether you are 38, approaching it, past it, or simply in
a season of deep transformation—this letter is for you.
Every lesson you've lived, every victory you've tasted,
every quiet shift within your spirit has led you to this
moment with purpose.

You no longer have anything to prove.
You are enough.
You are whole.
You are here by divine design.

Now is the time to step fully into the version of yourself
you've been steadily growing toward—
the healed version,
the grounded version,
the aligned and intentional version,
the version of you who keeps showing up, even when
the journey is heavy.

You are allowed to evolve.
You are allowed to pause.
You are allowed to redirect and begin again without shame.
Your timing is divine, even when your path feels unpredictable.

Release the guilt for what you didn't know before.
Forgive yourself for the moments you doubted your own light.
Honor the resilience that carried you through seasons no one else saw.
You are becoming—and you have earned every part of who you are rising into.

Let this truth settle into your bones:

I will not shrink.
I will not dim my brilliance.
I will not question my voice, my path, or my power.

I am stepping into my fullness with clarity and courage.

Every seed you plant in this season is sacred.
Your dreams, your intentions, your healing, your prayers—
they are taking root.
Doors are opening.
Peace is finding its way to you.
Alignment is meeting you exactly where you stand.

Be proud of this version of yourself.

You survived for this moment.

You healed for this moment.

Now you get to rise—

with strength, with softness, with purpose, and with truth.

Affirmation:
"In this season, I walk in power, peace, and purpose. I release doubt and fully embody the healed, radiant, and unstoppable version of myself."

Day 39

You Are in Divine Alignment"

Dear Beloved Soul,

Today is not just another day in your journey — it is divine alignment. The timing, the numbers, the progress you've made... none of it is random. It's confirmation that you are exactly where you're meant to be.

This moment is God's gentle whisper saying, " Keep going. I'm with you."

You've been showing up with intention — even on the days when your emotions felt heavy, your body felt tired, or your mind felt unsure. You've prayed, reflected, healed, and remained consistent. That discipline is sacred, and it has not gone unnoticed.

You are not behind.
 You are not lost.
 You are being guided — step by step, breath by breath.

The healing you're doing is reaching deeper than the wounds ever did. You are becoming the safe space you once longed for. You are becoming the strength you needed. You are becoming the peace you prayed for.

Let today remind you that your journey is spiritual, intentional, and generational.
 You are healing your past.
 You are honoring your present.
 You are preparing your future.

Everything is aligning — your spirit, your purpose, your steps.
 You are in divine alignment.

I am in divine
alignment.
My steps are ordered,
my heart is healing,
and my future is
unfolding *beautifully.*

Day 40

The View from Here"

Dear Beautiful Soul,

Look at how far you've come.
 Forty days of commitment.
 Forty days of truth-telling.
 Forty days of standing face-to-face with the parts of
yourself that needed love, honesty, and grace.

You have walked through uncomfortable emotions. You
have faced memories that once felt heavy. And through
it all, you've refused to let silence or shame have the
final say.

There is something sacred about showing up for
yourself — especially on the days when you felt tired,
uncertain, or overwhelmed. The version of you
emerging now is rooted, steady, and far more free than
before. You may not have every answer yet, but you do
know this: you've come too far to ever go backward.

You have built something new inside of you —
 something strong,
 something grounded,
 something unshakeable.

Today, you breathe deeper. Not because life is suddenly perfect, but because you have learned how to stop carrying everything alone. You chose healing... and healing chose you back.

Take a moment to thank God, the universe, and your own resilient spirit for guiding you — even when the path felt dim. There is a quiet strength holding you now, the kind that keeps you anchored through every storm.

The view from here is different.
You can see your growth.
You can feel your light.
You can recognize the version of you who refused to give up.

And you are still rising.

Affirmation:
"I honor how far I've come. I am healing in real time, and I trust the future I'm walking into."

Day 41

I No Longer Shrink"

Dear Beautiful Becoming,

You are no longer shrinking to fit places you've outgrown.
You are no longer silencing your truth to keep a peace that was never yours to hold.
You are no longer questioning whether you deserve joy, rest, or love — you know now that you do.

Day by day, your courage is becoming louder than your fear. And even when doubt whispers or old wounds rise to the surface, you meet them with grace and truth:
I am healing. I am becoming. I am worthy of more.

The past no longer dictates your pace.
It may teach you; it may strengthen you, but it does not define who you are becoming. You've walked through moments you once believed would break you, and now your presence in this season is evidence of your resilience and your rebirth.

Be gentle with yourself as you continue forward. You are not racing to arrive — you are unfolding, layer by layer, into your most authentic self. And that version of you is more than enough.

Affirmation:

"I honor my growth. I do not shrink to fit comfort zones—I rise to meet my purpose. I am free, expanding, and becoming EVERYTHING, I was created to be."

Day 42

"I Deserve Peace Without Apology"

Dear Beautiful Soul,

Today, I want you to breathe deeply and exhale the weight of over-explaining. You don't owe anyone an explanation for your peace, your rest, or your silence. You don't have to perform or push just to feel worthy. You already are.

You've carried so much on your shoulders, often without rest, and still gave to others even when you were barely holding on. But today, let this truth sink in: you deserve peace simply because you exist. Not because you worked hard enough. Not because you proved anything. Not because you were strong.
Just because you are.

You're learning how to protect your spirit — not out of bitterness, but out of love. You're releasing things that drain you, people who confuse you, and cycles that once kept you stuck. And in doing so, you're planting the roots of freedom.

Let go of the guilt that rises when you choose yourself. Let go of the urge to justify why you're unavailable, uninterested, or simply exhausted. The peace you're seeking is your birthright — and it no longer needs permission.

Keep healing. Keep choosing you. Keep honoring your limits without guilt.

Affirmation:
"I deserve peace, and I claim it unapologetically. I no longer over-explain my boundaries or my rest. I am worthy of softness, stillness, and joy."

Day 43

"Grace in the Pressure"

Dear Beautiful Soul,

There are seasons where life places weight on your shoulders—one challenge after another—almost daring you to break. Yet here you are, still standing, still showing up, still doing your best in a world that doesn't often pause for your struggles. That alone is proof of the strength within you.

Pressure doesn't just reveal where you feel stretched—it also reveals who you are at your core. And your core is built from something unshakable: faith, resilience, and a will that refuses to quit. You are not lost. You are in motion. Even when the path feels slow or heavy, every step you take is progress.

You may feel unseen at times, but you are not overlooked. The prayers you whisper, the hopes you carry, the responsibilities you balance—none of it goes unnoticed. Divine alignment often happens quietly, through subtle shifts, inner clarity, or unexpected support. Trust that the universe is already working on your behalf in ways you cannot yet see.

If you've been feeling stretched thin or restless, it's not because you're failing—it's because you're growing.

Breakthroughs often come after the pressure, not before it. You are being prepared, strengthened, and positioned for something greater.

So, pause. Breathe. Release the weight you don't have to carry alone. You've planted seeds with your faith, your effort, and your consistency.

Now allow the harvest to come.

Affirmation:
"Even in uncertainty, I am supported. I am surrounded by divine provision, peace, and clarity. I rise with strength, and I am never alone."

Day 44

"I Am a Safe Place for Myself"

Dear Soul in Bloom,
There is a deep peace in learning to be your own
sanctuary. In the quiet moments—when the world feels
loud or people misunderstand you—you can still return
to yourself and feel safe. You've been walking through a
season that required you to trust your own spirit, and
you've done just that. Every act of self-care, every
boundary honored, every time you chose healing over
hiding... you built safety from the inside out.

You no longer need to explain why you need rest,
solitude, joy, or stillness. You've earned all of it. You
deserve a life that doesn't feel like survival—a life with
laughter, music, softness, and fresh beginnings.
And today, as you clean your space and let your
favorite songs fill the room, remember: you're not just
tidying your home... you're clearing space for more of
you.
More light.
More love.
More truth.
More peace. You've carried yourself through more than

most will ever know. Keep nurturing this safe place within—it is your divine right, and it will carry you far.

Affirmation:
" *I am a safe, sacred space for myself. I choose peace, protect my energy, and honor the light within me.*"

Day 45

"I Am Not Who They Said I Was"

Dear Beautiful Soul,
 Today, remember this sacred truth: you are not the names, labels, or judgments others placed on you. You are not the stories spoken about you in rooms you never entered, nor the misunderstandings filtered through someone else's wounds. Those were reflections of their limitations—not your identity.

You've survived experiences that would have crushed others. You've poured love into places that did not pour back. You've extended grace even when you were exhausted. That doesn't make you weak—it makes you resilient, compassionate, and divinely strengthened. Every attempt to break you only revealed how deeply God has covered and restored you.

Let today be the day you shake off every label—too much, too emotional, too strong, too sensitive, too bold—and declare:
" I am not who they said I was. I am who God says I am."
 Worthy. Whole. Chosen. Becoming.

Your identity lives in your truth, not their perception.

Affirmation:

" I release every false label placed on me. I am evolving into my true, divine self—whole, worthy, and unstoppable."

Day 46

My Joy Is Sacred"

Dear Beautiful Soul,

There is a sound rising from within you today — a sound of victory. A vibration of praise that speaks louder than fear, louder than doubt, louder than anything that has ever tried to silence your spirit. Something in you is shifting, awakening, and expanding, and it is beautiful to witness.

You're entering a season where you're not merely surviving anymore — you're beginning to thrive. Your joy has weight. Your peace has presence. Your spirit is being watered in ways that are transforming you from the inside out.

You have been faithful to your healing.
 You have been consistent, even when heaviness lingered.
 You have stayed committed, even when clarity felt far away.

That is not small — that is sacred.

Today, allow the feeling of renewal to rise in you without apology. Let the music lift you. Let the joy keep you. Let God guide you into every step of this new chapter.

Remember this truth:

Your light is undeniable.
 Your purpose is real.
 Your joy is your resistance.
 And your healing is your birthright.

You are not who you were — and that is something to celebrate.
 You are becoming everything you were meant to be: rooted, radiant, and rising.

Affirmation:
"My joy is sacred. My healing is in motion. I walk boldly in the rhythm of grace."

Day 47

Dear Evolving Soul,

Today, pause and remember this truth: you are doing better than you think. Healing doesn't always announce itself. Sometimes it's quiet. Sometimes it's the soft resilience you show when you choose peace over chaos, grace over frustration, and faith over fear.

Even on the still days, healing is at work.

You are living proof that storms pass and seeds grow. Every challenge you've walked through has shaped you—deepening your wisdom, expanding your compassion, and strengthening your faith. You're no longer fighting to be seen. You're learning that your presence carries power even when your voice is gentle.

There is a divine rhythm awakening in you.
 A deeper tuning.
 A sacred alignment.

God is not only moving around your life—He is moving within it. And even when the path ahead feels unclear, your steps are guided. You are being led into a version of yourself that isn't just healed, but whole.

You are becoming the version of you that thrives.
 The version that shines without shrinking. The version

that walks in purpose and refuses to dim your own light.

Your story is sacred ground.

 Honor it. Continue writing it. Continue becoming.

Affirmation:
"I am stepping into wholeness. I release fear, I receive grace, and I honor the sacred journey shaping me."

Day 48

To Every Soul That's Still Standing"

Dear Soul,

You made it to today — and that alone is a victory.

This is for the souls who smile while healing silently...
For the ones who cry, yet still show up for others...
For the ones learning to believe in themselves again
after being torn apart...

I see you.
I honor you.
I understand you.

Healing is not always graceful. Some days it's messy.
Some days it's quiet. Some days it feels like nothing at
all. But still — it is holy. Every breath you take after
heartbreak is sacred. Every time you rise when life has
knocked you down is proof of the strength stitched into
your spirit.

If your heart feels bruised, your mind overwhelmed, or
your soul discouraged, hear this truth:

You are not weak.
You are not forgotten.
You are not alone.

You are becoming something powerful — something refined by fire, protected by grace, and held by Heaven itself. You are not just healing for you; you are healing for the ones who came before you and the ones who will come after you.

Your resilience is a lighthouse.
 Your rising is a testimony.
 Your light gives someone else permission to hope again.

So today, may your healing ripple outward like waves — touching someone who is on the edge of giving up. May your glow be a spark in another's darkness. And may you remember that even shattered pieces can reflect the brightest light.

You are sacred.
 You are healing.
 You are rising.

Affirmation for the Soul Collective:
"My healing is holy, and my journey inspires others to rise. I am a vessel of light, love, and restoration — touching lives simply by being me."

Day 49

Dear Divine Timing,

I trust you. Even when I don't understand you, I trust you. There were seasons when I questioned your pace—moments I thought you were late, too early, or not moving at all. But now I see the truth: every delay protected me, every detour redirected me, and every pause created space for me to grow.

I've learned that what's meant for me will never miss me. Healing doesn't follow a clock. Love, purpose, peace — they don't arrive on deadlines. They arrive when I am prepared to receive them, and you, Divine Timing, always know when that moment has come.

I release the pressure to rush. I release the need to compare. I trust that everything my soul needs is already on its way, and it will meet me at the exact moment I'm ready.

So today, I breathe.
 I pause.
 I move forward in faith — knowing that I am not behind, not delayed, not overlooked. I am exactly where I'm meant to be.

Affirmation :
"I trust the timing of my life. I am not late. I am not behind. I am aligned with the rhythm of divine order."

Day 50

Dear Beautiful Soul,

Fifty days.
 Fifty letters.
 Fifty moments of returning to yourself — piece by piece, breath by breath, truth by truth.

Today, I honor who I am and who I am becoming.
 The strength I didn't know I had.
 The courage I continue to uncover.
 The grace that keeps finding me, even in the quiet places.

Every scar is a sentence.
 Every breakthrough is a paragraph.
 Every new choice is a chapter.

I release the weight that was never mine to carry — the guilt, the shame, the expectations, the unspoken debts.
 I return to myself with softness, with compassion, with honesty.

There is holiness in every tear shed.
 There is beauty in every rising.
 There is purpose in every pause.
 There is power in every breath that refuses to give up.

Today, I celebrate my heart. Today, I walk in truth. Today, I stand in becoming. I am not broken, I am unfolding.

I honor how
far I've come.

I celebrate
who I am.

I trust the
person I'm
becoming.

Day 51

Dear Beautiful Soul,

Fifty-one days of showing up — through storms, through questions, through quiet victories no one else has seen. That alone is a miracle wrapped in strength, discipline, and grace.

Today, remember this truth: you are not healing to return to who you once were.
You are healing to become someone more whole, more aligned, and more aware of your divine purpose.

Layer by layer, you have released guilt, fear, doubt, and the weight of pain that was never meant to define you. Each day, you choose not to run from your hurt, but to move through it with courage.
That is sacred work.
That is generational transformation.
That is love in motion.

Even when the path feels uncertain, even when the process feels heavy, you are still planting seeds. Healing isn't always a loud breakthrough; often it is a quiet decision — to breathe through the tears, to stay present, to trust what you cannot yet see.
That is where your power grows: silently, steadily, faithfully.

So today, honor the tears that softened you, the stillness that centered you, the questions that deepened you, and the breakthroughs that lifted you. You are becoming someone the world truly needs — a soul who leads with love, insight, and purpose.

Keep your heart open and your vision wide.
 Miracles have a way of arriving right on time.

Affirmation:
 " I am not who I was— I am who I'm becoming. My healing is divine, MY GROWTH is unstoppable, and every step I take is guided by grace, power, and purpose."

Day 52

Breakthrough Is My Birthright"

Dear God,

Today, I come before You not just as someone in need, but as a soul who believes in divine turnaround. I have been planting, watering, waiting, and holding on — and even on the days when I grow weary, I choose to hope. I pray for breakthrough, not only in my finances, but in my heart, my home, and my relationships.

I pray for overflow where there has been lack.
 I ask for clarity where confusion once lived.
 I seek love that is sacred, intentional, and safe — not temporary, not surface-level, not wrapped in illusion.

You know my heart.
 You see the tears no one else witnesses.
 You've watched me give, grow, stretch, and surrender on this healing journey.
 Please align me with people, opportunities, and outcomes that carry Your fingerprints.

I release anything that drains my spirit or distracts me from my purpose.
 I will not settle for connections that leave my soul empty.

Help me stay grounded in my worth, because the breakthrough I desire begins with how I honor myself.

Today, I choose faith over fear.
Boundaries over desperation.
Purpose over patterns.
And belief that something greater is unfolding — even when I cannot yet see it.

Breakthrough is not a distant miracle.
It is my birthright.
And I receive it now.

Amen.

Affirmation :
"I am aligned with divine breakthrough — in my finances, my family, and my relationships. I attract love that sees my soul, honors my worth, and meets me with intention. I welcome what is sacred, steady, and true.

Day 53

Multiplied Strength, Unshakable Belief"

Dear Divine Me,

Today, I rise with a heart full of gratitude and a spirit
glowing with expectancy. I am not who I was yesterday,
and I welcome the evolution that each new day brings.
With every sunrise, I become more rooted in my power,
more certain in my path, and more aligned with the
blessings already set in motion for me.

There is a rhythm to my healing — a divine cadence that
guides my steps.
I no longer doubt the process.
I trust it.
My mind is calm.
My spirit is alert.
My heart is open.

I am walking toward everything meant for me.
I release fear.
I release delay.
I release disbelief.

In their place, I embrace strength, provision, clarity,
and divine alignment. Today, I celebrate all the
abundance I have — and all the abundance on its way to

me. Love flows to me. Resources flow to me. Peace flows through me.

This chapter of my life is different because I am different.
 I am aware.
 I am awakened.
 I am advancing.

I will no longer shrink to fit places I've outgrown.
 I was created for more — and now I walk like I know that deep in my soul.

Today, I shine without apology.
 I am grateful for this strength.
 I am grateful for this clarity.
 I am grateful for myself.

Affirmation:
"With every sunrise, my strength multiplies. I walk in divine timing, and all things align for my highest good."

Day 54

I Receive What Aligns with My Soul"

Dear Divine Flow,

Today, I give thanks for the blessings already on their way to me. I no longer chase, force, or beg. What is meant for my soul arrives in perfect timing. I am no longer available for chaos, confusion, or inconsistent energy. I am rooted in clarity, grounded in peace, and elevated by love.

I honor my healing.
 I honor my journey.
 Everything I've lived through has shaped me into a stronger, wiser, and more intentional version of myself. The doors that didn't open were protection. The people who left were redirection. The silence in between was a sacred pause — a moment for me to reflect, reset, and rise.

Today, I make space for more joy, more laughter, more deep breaths, more aligned connections, more ease, and more abundance. I release what drains me and open my heart to what fuels me.

I receive with open arms — not just anything, but only what aligns.
 Only what honors my boundaries.

Only what recognizes my value.
Only what speaks to my spirit and nourishes my mind.

I am no longer afraid of being too much or not enough.
I am exactly who I was created to be — and that is more than enough.

With every sunrise, my soul rises too.
With every blessing, I say thank you.

Affirmation :
"I am open to receive divine blessings that align with my soul, my peace, and my purpose."

Day 55

Alignment & Divine Positioning

Dear Divine Soul,

Today, I honor the power of alignment — the sacred flow that comes not from force but from surrender. I affirm that I am not behind. I am not late. I am exactly where I am meant to be. Every delay, every detour, every redirection has carried me to this moment of clarity, growth, and grace.

I release the urge to compare my path to anyone else's.
 I let go of the timelines the world has tried to place on me.
 My life is unfolding in divine order, and even when I cannot see the full picture, the universe is working on my behalf.

I trust that my name is being spoken in rooms I have not stepped into yet.
 I trust that doors are opening for me even as I rest.
 I trust that what is aligned for me cannot pass me by.

Today, I make peace with the process.
 I make peace with where I am.
 And I choose to align myself with the version of me who already knows they are worthy, supported, and destined for greatness.

I walk in faith.

 I breathe with intention. And I rise — in divine timing, in divine truth, and in divine power.

Affirmation:
"I am in divine alignment. Everything meant for me is already making its way to me. I trust the process, I trust my path, and I trust myself."

Day 56

Dear Divine Timing,

Today, I surrender to your rhythm. There are moments when I feel like I'm moving in circles, trying to build the life I see so clearly in my mind and spirit — but I'm learning that my journey isn't about rushing the process. It's about trusting it.

What I desire is not too much.
It is aligned with my purpose and my promise.

I desire peace.
I desire provision.
I desire joy.
I desire stability for myself and the people I love.
I desire a life that feels safe, fulfilling, and free.
I desire to be poured into the same way I pour into others.
I desire more than survival — I desire to thrive.

So even when my thoughts feel heavy and my heart feels restless, I remind myself that what is meant for me is already in motion. It is moving toward me, just as I am moving toward it. Every prayer whispered, every tear shed, every intention set — all of it has been seen, heard, and honored by God and by the Universe.

Today, I release the need to control the pace.
I breathe deeper. I speak gently to myself.
I open my hands to receive. I walk forward knowing I am supported, guided, and never alone. Everything I desire is finding its way to me. My life is unfolding in divine order — even when I cannot yet see the full picture.

Affirmation :
"What is meant for me is flowing toward me. I do not chase — I align. I trust the process, I honor the timing, and I receive all that is mine with peace and grace."

Day 57

Dear Beautiful Soul,

Today, I honor the fullness of who I am — every twist in my journey, every step forward, every lesson that has strengthened me, and every moment that has deepened my compassion. I rise knowing that I carry within me an endless well of resilience, purpose, and light.

I trust that what is meant for me is already finding its way.
I embrace each new day with gratitude, hope, and openness to the blessings unfolding in my life.
I honor the versions of me that survived, the versions of me that grew, and the version of me that continues to bloom.

I release past burdens, outdated fears, and lingering doubts.
I welcome joy.
I welcome clarity.
I welcome every opportunity aligned with my highest good.

May today remind you to be gentle with yourself and to celebrate every moment of growth. Cherish your journey, knowing that each thought, each emotion, each sunrise is another step toward the life your soul envisions.

Affirmation :

"I honor my journey, trust my unfolding, and welcome every blessing aligned with my highest good."

Day 58

You Are the Seed and the Sunlight"

Dear Divine Me,

Today, I honor the version of myself that dares to dream, dares to believe, and dares to rebuild from the ashes. I now understand something sacred — I am not just the seed. I am the sunlight too. I carry both the potential and the power to help it grow.

Even when life tried to bury me in darkness, I was quietly rooting. I was rediscovering myself, reclaiming myself, and loving myself back into wholeness. The light I offered others with ease — I now offer it to myself, freely and unapologetically.

I release the belief that I must shrink to be accepted.
I release the lie that my dreams are "too much."
Today, I water my own garden.
Today, I say yes to the becoming.

I do it without fear, because I know God planted me with purpose —on purpose.

I am living proof that healing is the glow-up.

Affirmation :
"I am both the vision and the vessel. I plant, I water, I bloom."

Day 59

Aligned With the Flow"

Dear Divine Soul,

Today, I stand in full alignment with the powerful current of life. I am no longer resisting what is meant for me, nor chasing what has already fulfilled its purpose. I am learning to flow — not from passivity, but from deep, sacred trust.

Every prayer I've released into the universe has been heard.
Every tear, every laugh, every seed planted in the unseen is beginning to bloom.
The shifts may feel subtle, but they are real. Something is happening. The energy around me is moving, rearranging, guiding me toward every blessing that matches my truth.

There is no room for desperation when I know I am deserving.
There is no room for doubt when I carry the proof — my breath, my survival, my growth.

I see now how life supports me when I stop trying to control each step and instead move with intention, peace, and expectancy.

I am no longer waiting for abundance.
I am abundance.
I walk like it, speak like it, think like it.
I trust the process even when the full picture hasn't formed, because my faith is louder than my fear.

Today, I release the urge to "figure it all out."
I choose instead to feel my truth, my alignment, my becoming.
I trust that my consistency is opening doors I don't even know exist yet.

And that's okay.
I am exactly where I need to be.

Affirmation:
"I am aligned with divine flow. Abundance finds me effortlessly. I trust the process, I trust my path, and I am ready to receive."

Closing Reflection:

Abundance is not just coming — it already knows my name.
It knows my light, my journey, my resilience. It is drawn to my readiness, my gratitude, and my faith.

My consistency is sacred.
It is proof of how deeply I love myself — through fear, through doubt, through setbacks, and through breakthroughs.
I am building a rhythm with my healing that no one can take away.

I am proud of myself.
I am rewriting my story with every thought, every prayer, every step forward.

What I m doing is rare.
What I m doing is holy.
And the overflow will be undeniable.

Day 60

I Kept Going"

Dear Milestone Maker,

Sixty days ago, I made a decision — a sacred vow to
show up for myself every day.
 To write.
 To speak life.
 To heal.
 To listen to my spirit more than my pain.

And here I am...
 Still here.
 Still rising.
 Still growing.
 Still believing.

I refuse to minimize this moment.
 This is divine.

Because some days were heavy.
 Some days I didn't feel like showing up.
 Some days I questioned everything—my strength, my
direction, my worth.
 But even then... I kept going.

And that is the miracle.
That is the healing.

I didn't have to be perfect — only present.
 I didn't need all the answers — only the courage to
keep asking.
 I didn't need to rush — only to trust.

Today, I honor every version of myself that brought me
here:
 the tired parts,
 the hopeful parts,
 the discouraged parts,
 the joyful parts.
 They all mattered.
 They all carried me.

This is not the end — it is an anchoring.
 A reminder that I can do anything with love,
commitment, and truth guiding me.
 My healing doesn't fade or expire — it expands.

So today, I celebrate this moment fully.
 With grace.
 With softness.
 With pride.

Because I kept going.
 And that changes everything.

Affirmation :

"I kept going. I honor my journey, I celebrate my strength, and I am proud of how far I've come. I welcome what's ahead with faith and open arms."

Day 61

Dear Beautiful Soul,

Today, I lean into a faith that doesn't ask how, when, or why.
I trust.
I believe.
I surrender.

With the innocence of a child, I step into this day expecting good to find me, surround me, and stay with me. I refuse to let past disappointments dim my hope. Instead, I allow my heart to remain light, open, and full of quiet anticipation. I remember that miracles don't require logic — they only require belief.

My joy is no longer tied to what I can control. It rises from the knowing that I am covered, guided, and chosen. Every step I take today moves me away from fear and closer to fulfillment. Every door that opens, every delay, every redirection — it's all working for me, not against me.

I am safe to hope again.
I am free to believe again.
I deserve to witness the beautiful outcomes my heart has whispered in prayer.

Today, I choose to smile for no reason, to laugh from my belly, and to live as though everything I've asked for is already here. Because in spirit — it is.

 It's already mine.

Affirmation:
"I walk in childlike faith — believing without fear, receiving without limits. Today, everything is working in my favor."

Day 62

Dear Self,

Today, I honor the light within me — the light that has carried me through storms, disappointments, and silent battles no one else ever knew existed. I acknowledge that every step of this journey has been a choice: a choice to love myself more deeply, to trust my own worth, and to stay aligned with the vision God placed in my heart.

I remind myself that I am not my past, nor am I defined by moments when I felt powerless.
 I am the embodiment of resilience — a living testimony that even in the darkest nights, the soul can rise and shine again.

I walk forward knowing that what is meant for me will always align with me in divine timing.
 I do not chase — I attract.
 I do not fear — I trust.

Every word I speak over myself plants seeds for my tomorrow.
 So today, I choose words rooted in abundance, faith, and self-love.
 I choose to affirm my worthiness of joy, prosperity, peace, and overflow.

I am ready for the goodness that is already moving toward me.

I open my heart to receive it fully.

Affirmation :
"I radiate light, peace, and confidence. What is meant for me flows to me with ease, abundance, and divine timing."

Day 63

Dear Beautiful Soul,

Today, I honor the flow of divine favor in my life. Even when I can't see the full picture, I trust that God and the universe are still moving on my behalf. The quiet shifts, the unseen alignments, the unexpected opportunities — all of it is evidence that I am divinely guided and supported.

I release the need to control every detail and instead choose to trust the process. My steps are ordered. My path is blessed. My faith is not limited by my circumstances — it expands beyond what I can see, reaching into possibilities that only God can orchestrate.

Today, I choose to be fully present in my joy — unbothered by fear, untouched by doubt. My heart is open to receive the good that is coming, and I refuse to block my blessings through overthinking, worry, or second-guessing my divine worth. I am worthy. I am favored. I am loved—always, in all ways.

Affirmation :
"Every day, in ways I see and ways I don't, blessings and miracles unfold for me. I am aligned, I am protected, and I am ready to receive."

Day 64

Dear Beautiful Me,

Today, I rest in the knowing that my life is divinely aligned. The people, opportunities, and blessings meant for me will never pass me by — and whatever is not for me will fall away with grace. I release the urge to chase, force, or cling to what is already mine by divine right.

I am safe in my becoming.
I am protected on my journey.
I am supported by a God who opens doors no one can shut and closes doors that are not aligned with my highest good.
I do not have to fear the unknown, because the unknown is where miracles are already forming for me.

Even when my mind feels full, I choose peace.
Even when I don't have all the answers, I choose trust.
Even as seasons shift, I choose to believe that my steps are ordered and my path is blessed.

I am proud of myself for showing up every single day.
I am grateful for my resilience, my hope, and the faith that keeps pulling me forward.

Affirmation :
"What is for me will always find me. I trust divine timing and welcome my blessings with open arms."

Day 65

Dear Beautiful Soul,

Today, I walk as if everything I desire is already mine.
I release the need to question, doubt, or rush the process.
I trust that what is meant for me will never miss me, and I am aligned with every blessing already on its way.

My light is magnetic —
it draws in divine connections,
financial overflow,
joy,
peace,
and every form of abundance designed for my highest good.

I trust my journey because I am both the author of my story and the co-creator of my reality with God.
Nothing that is aligned for me will be withheld.
Nothing destined for me will pass me by.

Affirmation:
I am a magnet for success, joy, and abundance. My energy attracts only what is good, pure, and aligned with my highest self."

Day 66

Grand rising, Beautiful Soul.

Today, I walk boldly into my greatness — carrying faith as my armor and joy as my shield. Even when my heart wrestles with battles no one else can see, I choose to wear peace on my face and kindness in my actions. I smile not to hide my truth, but to reflect my unshakable belief that everything — the visible and the invisible — is working for my highest good.

I am bold enough to face challenges head-on.
 I am brave enough to keep my light shining when shadows try to creep in.
 I am luminous enough to inspire hope, love, and courage in others simply by being who I am.

Today, I will laugh from my soul, smile from my heart, and extend grace to myself and those around me. If storms arise beyond my control, I will remain rooted in positivity, knowing my faith is greater than any obstacle.

My steps are ordered.
 My spirit is strong.
 My presence carries light wherever I go.

Affirmation :

"I am bold, brave, and beautiful. I choose joy over fear, faith over doubt, and love over negativity. The unseen bends in my favor, and I walk confidently in my divine power."

Day 67

Dear Self,

Today, I honor the way I carry so much within me. I know what it feels like to smile on the outside while weathering a storm within, and I offer myself compassion for every moment I've had to be strong in silence.

Grief has walked beside me like a quiet shadow, but I refuse to let it dim the light of who I am becoming. I allow myself to feel without judgment — to honor the ache without letting it define me. I am learning that grief does not always mean darkness; sometimes it means love that hasn't found a place to rest yet.

Connections are a lifeline. I remind myself it is safe to lean into the people who see me, uplift me, and hold space for the parts of me I don't always show. I don't have to carry everything alone. My soul thrives in spaces where I can be both soft and supported.

Even in moments of heaviness, my motivation remains. Something inside me still whispers, rise. I rise because my purpose is bigger than my pain. I rise because even broken pieces can be arranged into something whole and beautiful. I rise because I am not done becoming.

So today, I embrace both truths:
 I can hurt and still heal.
 I can cry and still shine.
 I can break and still rebuild.

My spirit remains unshaken, and I honor every part of
my journey — the messy, the miraculous, and
everything in between.

Affirmation :
*"I honor my grief while choosing to shine. I am connected,
supported, and resilient — even when I feel broken inside."*

Day 68

Dear Self,

Today, I remind myself that healing is not about forgetting — it's about learning to carry my experiences with more grace and less heaviness. Grief has a way of arriving uninvited, slipping into my thoughts when I least expect it. But I give myself permission to feel it without shame. I do not have to be the strong one every moment of every day. There is freedom in that truth.

Connections remind me that I am never walking alone. The right people see beyond the surface — they nurture my spirit, honor my humanity, and remind me of my worth when my energy feels low. I open myself to connections that pour back into me, that feel mutual, honest, and rooted in genuine care.

My motivation may not always roar, but it is steady. Even when my heart feels heavy, something within me whispers, keep going. That whisper is evidence of my resilience. It is proof that I can hold both joy and sorrow, both light and shadow, both hope and uncertainty — and still choose forward movement.

Today, I honor my resilience. I release the pressure to hold myself together perfectly. I recognize strength not in how tightly I cling to composure, but in how deeply I continue to show up for myself, even when my spirit trembles.

Affirmation :
"I allow myself to feel, to heal, and to be held. My connections uplift me, my motivation sustains me, and my spirit remains unbreakable."

Day 69

Dear Self,

Today, I breathe into the space between what I've lost and what I'm becoming. Grief can feel like a weight pressing against my chest, but each breath I take is proof that I am still here — still capable of loving, growing, and opening myself to joy again.

Connections anchor me. I am learning to value the people who see me beyond the mask, the ones who don't need me to be perfect in order to stay. It is safe to let others in, even when my insides feel tender or messy. True connections don't demand perfection — they welcome my truth.

Motivation rises within me as I remember why I continue forward. I am not only moving for myself, but for the legacy I am building — a legacy of strength, compassion, and faith. Even when I feel scattered inside, I remind myself that healing isn't a single moment. It's a collection of small victories, quiet courage, and steps taken even with trembling feet.

So today, I honor my process.
I can smile and still have tears waiting behind my eyes.
I can stumble and still be growing.
I can hurt and still be whole in spirit.

I am worthy of the blessings moving toward me, even in seasons of grief. I rise because it is in my nature to rise.

Affirmation :
"I am anchored in love, guided by purpose, and strong enough to rise through grief. I honor my process and keep moving forward."

Day 70

Dear Self,

Seventy days of showing up — even on the days when it felt impossible, even when your heart was heavy, even when the world asked more of you than you had to give. Today, I pause to honor that truth. I am proud of the commitment I've made to myself. Every word written, every tear shed, every affirmation spoken has been a seed planted in the garden of my healing.

Grief may still visit me, but I no longer see it as a weakness or a setback. It is the lingering echo of love, proof that my heart has cared deeply. And even on the days when I've smiled while holding pain quietly inside, I now understand — that is strength, not pretense. That is courage.

Connections continue to ground me. They remind me that life is not meant to be navigated alone. I welcome relationships that uplift, inspire, and hold space for both my laughter and my silence. I deserve that kind of nourishment.

My motivation grows in ways both subtle and profound. It's not always loud; sometimes it's simply waking up and choosing to try again. But even the quietest efforts count. Those small choices prove my resilience just as much as my greatest victories.

So today, I celebrate myself — not for being perfect, but for being present... for being willing... for being resilient. I am a living testimony of strength. And no matter what I face, my light will continue to shine.

Affirmation :
"I celebrate 70 days of courage and growth. I am strong, I am loved, and I am worthy of every blessing unfolding in my life."

Day 71

Dear Self,

Today, I acknowledge the adversaries in my life — not just people, but the doubts, fears, patterns, and obstacles that have tried to hold me back. Adversity shows up in many forms, yet with every challenge I rise stronger and more aware of who I am becoming.

I will not be defined by the forces working against me. I will be defined by the way I rise above them.

Every setback has pushed me toward a comeback. Every moment of resistance has revealed my strength. Every obstacle has sharpened my clarity and deepened my resilience.

I am no longer afraid of challenges. I now understand that everything sent to shake me only confirms that I am rising into greater power. If I were not destined for greatness, I would not feel such resistance.

Connections matter even in the face of adversity. I lean into the people who uplift me, support me, and remind me of my truth. I create distance from those who drain my spirit or disrupt my peace. True support nourishes my soul, while negativity reminds me, I'm moving in the right direction.

My motivation remains unshaken.
Adversaries no longer intimidate me — they inform me.
They remind me of my purpose, my calling, and my divine protection.

So today, I walk forward with faith, courage, and an unbreakable spirit.
What is meant for me cannot be taken.
What is aligned with me cannot be blocked.

Affirmation:
"I rise above every adversary with strength, courage, and faith. What comes against me cannot stop what is destined for me."

Day 72

Dear Self,

Today, I choose to be real with myself. Life hasn't been easy — grief, adversaries, and silent battles have all tried to weigh me down. But look at me. I'm still here. I'm still standing. And that alone is proof that I am made of something unshakable.

There have been moments when I've smiled on the outside while crumbling on the inside.
That doesn't make me weak — it makes me human.

But today, I choose more than just holding it together.
Today, I choose release.

I give myself permission to feel what I feel without apology.
To cry if I need to.
To let the heaviness leave my body instead of carrying it like a lifelong companion.
I deserve to feel light again.

Connections are waiting to pour love back into me.
I release the belief that I need to apologize for needing support.
It does not make me a burden — it makes me real.
I open myself to love, to comfort, to motivation, and to

the people who remind me that I don't have to walk alone.

And when life tests me, I remember this truth:
Every tear, every struggle, every setback is shaping me into an unstoppable force.
My story is not over.
My joy will return.
My peace will find me.
My heart will feel whole again.

So, I keep going — not because everything is perfect, but because greatness is written all over me.
I am becoming more myself every day.

Affirmation:
"I release what no longer serves me and welcome peace, love, and joy. I am unstoppable, unshakable, and divinely guided."

Day 73

Dear Self,

Today marks a new chapter in this journey. I have walked through grief, faced adversaries, leaned into meaningful connections, and kept my motivation alive even when my heart felt heavy. That alone is worth celebrating.

Day by day, I am proving to myself that healing is not about perfection — it is about persistence.
 It is about showing up when my spirit is tired.
 It is about breathing through moments I once thought would break me.
 It is about honoring the quiet courage that keeps me moving forward, even when no one else sees the effort.

Grief may still knock at my door, but I refuse to let it consume my story.
 I can honor the pain without living in it.
 I can carry the memory without carrying the weight.

Adversaries may rise, but I am covered, guided, and protected.
 What is meant for me cannot be taken.
 What is aligned with me cannot be blocked.

Today, I breathe deeply into the truth:
 I am still here.

I am still growing.
I am still becoming.

My light has not dimmed — it has expanded through every trial, every tear, and every moment of resilience. I step forward knowing the best chapters of my life are still unfolding before me.

Affirmation :
"I honor my journey, I trust my process, and I walk forward in strength and grace. My best days are still ahead of me."

Day 74

Dear Self,

Today, I honor the way I continue to stand strong, even when life sends unexpected twists my way. My journey hasn't been simple, yet here I am — still rising, still growing, still holding onto my light.

The challenges I face are not signs of weakness.
They are reminders of my resilience.
Every delay, every denial, and every obstacle is transforming into evidence of my endurance.
I am not defined by what was withheld from me — I am defined by how I rise and respond.

I give myself permission to feel good about the blessings unfolding around me.
The progress of the people I love — including my child — reminds me that hope is alive, and that even in the midst of trials, joy still finds its way through. Their growth is a reflection of my prayers, my faith, and the love I pour out every day.

Today, I release the weight of what others failed to do, say, or uphold.
Their choices are not my burden.
Their actions are not my responsibility.
My healing, my faith, and my persistence are what carry me forward.

So, I stand tall, grounded in the truth that everything meant for me will find me — in perfect timing, in perfect alignment, and with undeniable clarity.

Affirmation :

"I release the weight of what others failed to do for me. I walk forward with strength, faith, and clarity, trusting that what is mine will always find me."

Day 75

Dear Self,

Seventy-five days.
 Seventy-five moments of choosing myself.
 Seventy-five steps into healing, faith, and resilience.

Today, I pause not to replay what was hard — but to celebrate how far I have come.

I honor the strength it took to show up for myself day after day.
 I honor every tear, every prayer, every affirmation, and every breakthrough.
 Even in the moments I felt like I was falling apart, I rose again.
 That is worth celebrating.

This is my reset moment.
 A shift.
 A renewal.
 A breath of fresh strength.

From this day forward, I release the weight of old disappointments and walk into a season of clarity, joy, and new beginnings.
 My spirit is refreshed.
 My heart is open.
 My path is glowing with possibility.

I give myself permission to feel joy without guilt, to embrace peace without hesitation, and to celebrate myself without apology.

Today, I lift my head high and declare:
"I am proud of me."

Celebration Mantra

Whisper it... write it... say it boldly.

I am proud of my journey.
I celebrate my resilience, my growth, and the
unstoppable light within me."

Call-and-Response Mantra

Say it with power:

You say: Have I shown up for myself every day?"
You answer: Yes! I am here, I am strong, I am unstoppable!"

You say: Am I proud of my journey?"
You answer: Absolutely! I celebrate my growth, my resilience, and my light!"

You say: Am I ready for what s next?"
You answer: Yes! I am renewed, recharged, and ready for blessings beyond my imagination!"

Repeat whenever you need a spark.

Visual Imagery Exercise

Close your eyes and see this:

You are standing in a wide-open field, sunlight warm on your skin.

Around you, 75 glowing lanterns float upward — each one representing a day you chose yourself.

As they rise, the sky fills with light.

You smile, knowing you created this moment with your courage and consistency.

Ahead of you, a path lined with blooming flowers stretches forward — your next chapter, illuminated and waiting for you.

DAY 75

I celebrate my resilience,
my growth, and my light.
I am renewed, recharged,
and ready for the blessings
unfolding in my life.

Day 76

Dear Healing Journey,

Today, I embrace the beauty of stillness. Even when the day feels ordinary or quiet, I trust that healing is still happening within me. Progress doesn't always arrive with fireworks or grand breakthroughs — sometimes it shows up in the soft peace that settles over me after releasing what no longer serves my spirit.

I am learning that every day carries value, no matter how it unfolds. Whether I move quickly or take my time, whether I achieve much or simply rest, I know I am still worthy, still growing, still transforming. My journey is not measured by how much I accomplish, but by the love, awareness, and intention I bring into each moment.

Today, I honor the small victories — the breaths that calm me, the choices that free me, the faith that keeps me grounded. I honor myself for continuing forward, even when the steps are quiet and gentle.

I am exactly where I am meant to be.

Affirmation:
"I honor my journey in every form — quiet or bold, still or active. Each day, I am healing, growing, and walking in divine alignment."

Day 77

Dear Self,

Today, I celebrate the renewal I feel within. My spirit is refreshed, and I am grateful for the strength rising up in me. Even after everything I have faced, I stand here with my heart open to love, to peace, and to new opportunities. I honor my healing journey because every step brings me closer to the life I deserve — one filled with joy, abundance, and divine alignment.

I remind myself that the past no longer holds power over me. What lies ahead is brighter, greater, and overflowing with promise. I am proud of the courage it takes to keep showing up for myself every single day. My consistency, my faith, and my hope are the keys unlocking the blessings designed for me.

Today, I walk in renewal, knowing that I am guided, protected, and deeply loved.

Affirmation :
"I am renewed in spirit, strengthened in purpose, and aligned with the abundant blessings flowing into my life."

Day 78

Beloved One,

This morning, before the world fully awoke, you were called into stillness. In those early hours, when your thoughts began to stir, you chose not to drown in them — but to rise, breathe, and pray. That choice was not small; it was sacred.

In the quiet, you met God.
In that space, you were reminded:
You are not alone.
Your steps are ordered.
Your prayers are heard.

Even when the mind feels restless, the spirit knows exactly where to go. You turn inward, you turn upward, and you trust that all things are working together for your good. The favor you seek is already unfolding, even in the unseen. What felt like sleeplessness may have been divine alignment — a gentle reminder that God's timing is not confined to clocks or calendars.

Today, carry peace with you.
Let the memory of that guided stillness be your anchor. Whatever comes, you are not walking through it empty — you are moving with the strength of your faith, the clarity of your spirit, and the assurance that breakthrough is drawing near.

Affirmation:

"I am aligned with divine timing. Even in restless moments, I am guided, protected, and favored. Everything is working together for my highest good."

Day 79

Dear Beautiful Soul,

This morning, my spirit feels a bit unsettled, and I am reminded that life often brings moments of discomfort and uncertainty. Challenges can appear without warning, and sometimes the weight of everything can feel heavy. Yet even in those moments, I remember this truth:

I am not walking this path alone.

There is a Greater Presence — a Source of strength and light — guiding me, holding me, and carrying me forward when my steps feel unsure.

Healing, I'm learning, is not about denying pain or pretending everything is perfect. Healing is the courage to face what hurts while still choosing hope. It is trusting that renewal is possible even when the road feels long. Trouble may show up, but so does grace. So does strength. So does the quiet reminder that help is always near.

To the soul reading these words:
 Your journey matters.
 Your struggle does not make you less worthy.
 It makes you human — and it connects you to all of us walking our own paths of growth and restoration.

You are not alone.

Peace is possible.

Healing belongs to you, too.

Affirmation :

"I am never without strength, guidance, or love. No challenge is greater than the light within me. Healing flows through me, restores me, and uplifts those around me."

Day 80

Dear Beautiful Soul,

Today, I celebrate the beauty of new beginnings. Life has a way of carrying yesterday's struggles, regrets, or disappointments into today, but every sunrise whispers the same gentle truth:

You can begin again.

New beginnings don't erase the past — they transform it. They remind us that we are not defined by what tried to break us, but by the courage it took to rise again. Every moment is a fresh invitation to release what no longer serves you and step forward with hope, faith, and grace.

So, if you are reading this today, hold this truth close:
 Your story is far from over.
 Renewal is always within reach.
 The same light that rises for me rises for you.

Take a deep breath — it is proof that you have been given another chance. You are worthy of fresh starts. You are worthy of peace. You are worthy of healing.

Affirmation:
 Each day is a fresh start, filled with possibility and grace. I release what no longer serves me and welcome the new with courage, faith, and hope. My journey is living proof that renewal is always within reach."

Day 81

Dear Beautiful Soul,

Today, I honor the strength that comes from stillness. The world often encourages us to keep moving, keep pushing, keep proving — but healing has taught me a different truth:

There is power in pausing.
There is growth in silence.
There is renewal in rest.

Stillness is not weakness — it is sacred space. It is the moment we can hear our own heart, feel our breath, and remember that even when we are not "doing," we are still becoming. In stillness, wounds are tended, peace is restored, and clarity begins to rise gently within us.

So, if today feels heavy, give yourself permission to be still.
You do not have to have all the answers.
You do not have to fight every battle at once.
You do not have to earn your worth through constant motion.

Trust that even in your quiet moments, you are healing.
You are being held.

You are becoming.
You are enough.

Affirmation:
"Stillness restores me, strengthens me, and reconnects me to my inner peace. Even in quiet moments, I am growing, I am healing, and I am enough"

Day 82

Dear Beautiful Soul,

Today, I remind myself to embrace the journey. Healing is not a straight line, and growth doesn't always arrive in ways I expect. Some days feel like bold leaps forward; others feel like slow, quiet steps. But every part of the journey matters. Every step is shaping me into who I am becoming.

It's easy to look back at where I've been or look ahead at how far I still want to go — but peace lives in the present moment. Right here, right now, I am enough. The lessons, the pauses, the struggles, and the victories are all part of the beautiful story unfolding in my life.

And to you, dear soul, who may feel weary on your path:
Trust that the journey itself is sacred.
Even when you cannot see the finish line, know that each step carries purpose.
Healing is happening — in ways seen and unseen.

Keep walking with hope.
You are exactly where you need to be.

Affirmation:
"My journey is sacred. Every step, whether big or small, carries purpose and meaning. I embrace the process, trust my growth, and honor who I am becoming."

Day 83

Dear Beautiful Soul,

Today, I remind myself that detours and delays do not define me. Life doesn't always unfold according to my plans, and at times that reality can feel frustrating or discouraging. But even in those moments, I am learning this truth:

My worth is not diminished because things look different than I expected.
My journey is not weakened because the timing shifted.
My destiny is not denied because the path took a turn.

Every unexpected twist is part of a greater design.
What I see as a setback may actually be preparation.
What feels like lost time may be divine protection.
What seems like confusion may be the re-routing I didn't know I needed.

When I shift my focus from what I cannot control to the faith that carries me, peace returns — steady, grounding, and real.

And to you, dear soul, who may also feel thrown off course:
Hold on.
You are not behind.

You are not forgotten.

You are not lost.

The path you're on — even with its twists, pauses, and redirections — is still leading you toward growth, purpose, and healing.

Affirmation:

"Detours do not destroy my destiny. Every step, planned or unplanned, is part of my growth. I release frustration and walk in trust, peace, and purpose."

Grounding Affirmation:

"Even when things don't go as planned, I am still on the right path. I release the need to control every detail and trust that what is meant for me will not miss me. My peace is steady, my focus is strong, and my faith keeps me grounded."

Day 84

"Resilience in the Storm"

Dear Resilient One,

Today, I honor the strength that rises within me even when life feels like a storm. The winds may shake me, the rain may fall heavy, and the clouds may gather — but I will not break. Instead, I bend, I breathe, and I allow every storm to deepen my roots.

Every challenge I've faced has carried a lesson.
 Every hardship has stretched me in ways I once thought I could not endure.
 Yet here I am — still standing, still growing, still believing.

Storms are temporary.
 But the strength they awaken in me lasts forever.

To you who may be weathering your own storm:
 Trust that it will pass.
 You are stronger than you know.
 You may bend under the weight, but you will not break.

With every trial, you are being shaped, fortified, and prepared for greater days ahead.
 Your roots are deepening.

Your spirit is strengthening.

Your resilience is becoming unshakable.

Affirmation :

"No storm can shake the foundation of who I am. I bend, I grow, I rise — and I come out stronger every time."

Day 85

The Beauty of Becoming

Dear Beautiful Soul,

Today, I remind myself that growth is not always easy — but it is always worth it. Every challenge I've faced has been shaping me, stretching me, and guiding me closer to the person I am becoming.

Becoming isn't about perfection.
It's about progress.
It's about embracing the lessons, even when they arrive wrapped in discomfort or pain.
It's about trusting that what feels heavy right now is building a strength I will carry for the rest of my life.

To you who may feel tired or uncertain on your journey:
Take heart.
You are becoming too.
Every step — bold or small — is evidence of your growth.
You may not see the full picture yet, but one day you will look back and realize how beautifully you were being shaped all along.

You are unfolding in grace.
You are becoming in purpose.
You are blooming, even now.

Affirmation :

"I am beautifully becoming. Every challenge shapes me, every step grows me, and every season carries me closer to my purpose."

Day 86

Dear Healing Spirit,

Today, I remind myself that healing is not about reaching a finish line. It is not about having every wound closed or every question answered. Healing is a journey — a daily choice — a process of becoming whole in my own time and in my own way.

Some days, I feel the strength of my progress.
Other days, I feel the weight of my pain.
Both are valid.
Both belong.
Both are part of my healing.

I do not have to rush myself.
I do not have to force completion.
I only need to keep moving forward with faith, hope, and love.

To you who are healing too:
Give yourself grace.
You may not see it clearly, but every small step, every deep breath, every quiet act of courage is evidence that you are healing.

Progress may be quiet — but it is still powerful.

Affirmation :

"I am a work in progress, and that is enough. Every breath, every step, and every choice to keep going is part of my healing. I am growing, I am becoming, I am whole."

Day 87

Dear Unstoppable Spirit,

Today, I honor my feelings — even the ones that come wrapped in disappointment or unpleasant news. My emotions deserve space, and I allow myself to feel them without shame. But I also choose not to live in them. I choose to shift toward alignment, toward peace, toward faith.

That shift is strength.

That shift is growth.

That shift is faith in action.

I remind myself that my journey has never been in vain. Every tear, every setback, every trial has shaped me into someone stronger, wiser, and more compassionate. I refuse to see myself as broken. I see myself as becoming — becoming whole, becoming grounded, becoming powerful through every experience I've survived.

Life may test me, but I rise.

Darkness may surround me, but my light does not dim. I carry within me the unshakable truth that I was created with purpose — and no hardship can take that destiny away.

To you who may be walking your own path of struggle: Know this — you are greater than your pain.

Trouble may be present, but so is your resilience.
Fear may whisper, but so does your faith.
Every breath you take is proof that you are still here,
still fighting, still becoming.

Let today remind you that you are not defined by what
you've endured — but by how you continue to rise
through it.

Affirmation :
*"I am unbreakable, unstoppable, and unshaken. Every
challenge fuels my growth. I rise with power, stand in faith,
and live with purpose."*

Day 88

Dear Enduring Spirit,

Today, I celebrate the progress I have made and the strength that has carried me here. Eighty-eight days ago, I began this journey with hope, faith, and a determination to rise above my pain. Each letter, each affirmation, each moment of honesty has been a step forward — a seed planted in the garden of my healing.

But I know this is not the end.
 Healing is not something I "finish."
 It is a lifelong unfolding — a gentle, continuous becoming.

Every day I breathe, I have another chance to grow deeper in love, stronger in faith, and more grounded in peace. What I've begun on this journey is only the foundation of something greater.

To you who are reading this:
 Do not wait for a moment of "completion" before you celebrate yourself.
 Healing is not about reaching perfection — it is about choosing to rise, again and again, no matter what life brings.
 Every step matters.
 Every effort counts.
 Every breath you take in hope is victory.

I honor how far I've come.

I honor where I am.

And I open my heart to where I'm going next.

Affirmation :

"My healing is ongoing, and I embrace the journey ahead. Every step I take is progress. Every moment I choose hope is victory. I am proud of how far I've come, and excited for where I am going."

Day 89

Legacy of Healing"

Dear Lightbearer,

Day 89 — a number that reflects devotion, heart, and unwavering consistency. This is more than a milestone. It is a reminder that healing is a legacy, not a moment. And today, we step fully into that truth.

Your healing is not only for you.
 Every word you've written, every affirmation you've spoken, every quiet step you've taken toward wholeness sends ripples far beyond your own life. Your growth becomes strength for those connected to you, hope for those who feel unseen, and light for anyone navigating their own shadows.

This journey has taught something sacred:

When one soul heals, it gives others permission to believe that healing is possible, too.
 Pain loses its power when we stop hiding it and begin transforming it — into purpose, into testimony, into legacy.

To you, the soul reading these words:
 Your healing matters deeply.

Your resilience matters.
Your choice to keep going leaves a mark on the world.

We do not heal only for ourselves.
We heal for the generations coming after us.
We heal for the hearts searching for hope.
We heal for the collective rise of every soul determined
to break cycles and build something better.

You are part of something greater.
Your healing is your legacy.

Affirmation :
*"My healing creates a legacy of strength, love, and faith.
My journey inspires others to rise, just as I am rising."*

Day 90

Legacy. Becoming. Rising.

Dear Victorious Soul,

Today marks the completion of a 90-day journey —
90 days of reflection, honesty, courage, and
unwavering faith.

What began as a simple commitment to show up each
day became something far greater:
a reminder that healing expands beyond the self,
touching hearts and inspiring others to rise as well.

Ninety days ago, I made a choice:
to heal with intention,
to speak truth with courage,
to show up even when my spirit felt tired,
and to trust that every step carried purpose.

Through storms, I still found light.
Through weariness, I still chose to rise.
I embraced my wounds not as signs of defeat,
but as proof that I survived —
that I am still becoming —
and that nothing can stop the healing meant for me.

This letter does not mark an ending.
It marks an expansion.

Healing does not conclude on Day 90.
Healing breathes through every prayer whispered,
every affirmation spoken,
every boundary set,
every choice to rest,
every moment of rising after the fall.

We close this chapter not with finality,
but with gratitude for what it has shaped within us
and readiness for the chapters still waiting to bloom.

Healing is a legacy.
Growth is a testimony.
New beginnings are a promise.

We are not just healing —
we are becoming.
What tried to break us has shaped us into something
unshakable.
This is not the end of the journey —
it is the beginning of the rising.

Affirmation :
*"I am healed, whole, and walking boldly in my purpose.
This journey has strengthened me, but it does not limit me
— for I am still becoming, still rising, and still shining."*

Reflection Recap

What the Last 90 Days Have Taught Us

Healing is not a destination, but a sacred unfolding.

We possess strength beyond every storm we have faced.

Our voices carry power — not just for ourselves, but for every soul connected to us.

Faith, consistency, and love can transform pain into legacy. Rising once is courage; rising every day is transformation.

New Beginning Declaration

This is not the end of healing —
it is the continuation of rising.

From this day forward:
We walk in strength.
We move with purpose.
We shine with clarity.
We live as proof that healing is real, possible, and
transformative.

We carry this legacy of healing into every room,
every relationship, every season.
We are becoming the healed, the whole, the rising.

Celebratory Send-Off Note

90 days. 90 letters. 90 affirmations.

What started as a personal promise has grown into
something greater —
a legacy of faith, healing, and resilience.

This isn't the end...
it's the beginning of our rising.

Here s to healing.
Here s to growth.
Here s to new beginnings — we rise.

With gratitude and light,

—The Journey Continues

A Note from the Author

The Journey Continues

Ninety days ago, this journey began with a single intention:
to heal.
Not perfectly.
Not quickly.
But honestly.

One letter became many.
One affirmation became a way of life.
And day by day, something sacred unfolded — not just
within these pages, but within the heart behind them.

These 90 days are not an ending.
They are a doorway.

Healing doesn't stop at a milestone.
Growth doesn't disappear when the writing pauses.
Transformation doesn't wait for perfect conditions.

What you've done here — showing up, reflecting, speaking
life into yourself — is the foundation for everything you will
continue to become.

Through these letters, we learned that healing is a daily
choice, not a single moment; that resilience lives inside you
even when you don't feel strong; that your story carries
power even when you whisper it; that you are never alone on
this journey; and that becoming is a lifelong unfolding.

If you take nothing else from this book, take this:

You are worthy of the life you are building.
You are deserving of peace, love, joy, and abundance.
You are not behind. You are becoming.

And even on the days when you feel like you're starting over,
remember:

Starting over is also progress.
Pausing is also progress.
Gentleness with yourself is also progress.

As you step beyond Day 90, may you carry forward faith that
moves quietly but powerfully, hope that refuses to die,
courage that rises even in uncertainty, and love — for
yourself, for your journey, and for the beautiful becoming
unfolding within you.

This is not the end.
This is your next beginning.

Keep rising.
Keep healing.
Keep becoming.

With gratitude, grace, and endless belief in you,

— Keona Young

About the Author

Keona is a writer, mother, and healing storyteller whose journey through adversity sparked a transformative 90-day practice of daily letters and affirmations. What began as a private act of survival blossomed into a powerful healing path that touched others, revealing her natural gift for speaking life into the souls of those who need it most.
In a season marked by loss, transition, and emotional weight, she turned inward—choosing to write her way toward clarity, faith, and restoration. When she shared her early letters with someone in need and witnessed their emotional impact, Keona realized her words carried purpose beyond her own healing.
Rooted in authenticity, resilience, and unwavering belief in divine alignment, her work invites every reader to remember that they are not alone, that their story matters, and that healing is not only possible—it is transformative.
This is her first published collection, born from truth, inner strength, and the courage to keep becoming. Through her writing, Keona hopes to inspire others to rise, reclaim their light, and continue their own journey toward wholeness.

www.ingramcontent.com/pod-product-compliance
Lightning Source LLC
Chambersburg PA
CBHW021146130626
46554CB00005B/1686